Tasting

by Helen Frost

Consulting Editor: Gail Saunders-Smith, Ph.D.

Consultant: Eric H. Chudler, Ph.D.
Research Associate Professor
Department of Anesthesiology
University of Washington, Seattle

Pebble Books

an imprint of Capstone Press
Mankato, Minnesota

Pebble Books are published by Capstone Press
818 North Willow Street, Mankato, Minnesota 56001
http://www.capstone-press.com

Library of Congress Cataloging-in-Publication Data
Frost, Helen, 1949–
    Tasting/by Helen Frost.
    p. cm.—(The senses)
    Includes bibliographical references and index.
    Summary: Simple text and photographs describe and illustrate the sense
of taste. 6-27-01
    ISBN 0-7368-0385-8
    1. Taste—Juvenile literature. [1. Taste. 2. Senses and sensation.] I. Title.
II. Series: Frost, Helen, 1949– The senses.
QP456.F76 2000
612.8′7—dc21
                                       99-14306
                                         CIP

Note to Parents and Teachers

The Senses series supports national science standards for units related to behavioral science. This book describes and illustrates the sense of taste. The photographs support early readers in understanding the text. The repetition of words and phrases helps early readers learn new words. This book also introduces early readers to subject-specific vocabulary words, which are defined in the Words to Know section. Early readers may need assistance to read some words and to use the Table of Contents, Words to Know, Read More, Internet Sites, and Index/Word List sections of the book.

Table of Contents

Taste is one of your five senses. You use your tongue to taste.

Your tongue has tiny taste buds. Different taste buds detect the flavors in different foods.

Food touches your taste buds. Your taste buds send signals to your brain. Your brain understands the flavor you taste.

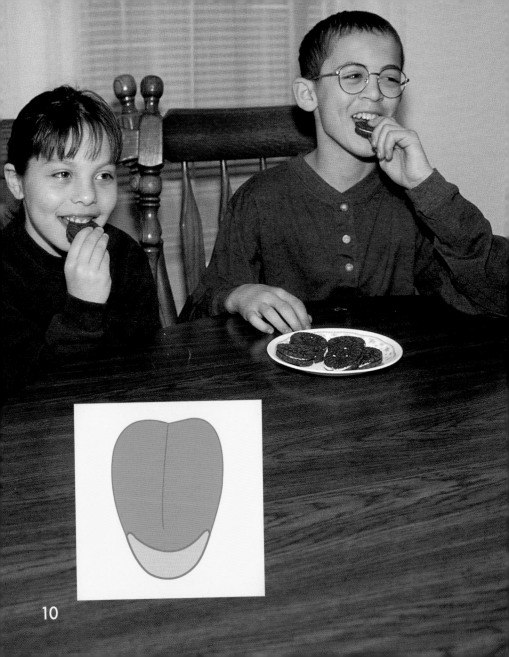

You taste sweet foods best on the front of your tongue. A cookie tastes sweet.

You taste salty foods best on the front and sides of your tongue. A pretzel tastes salty.

You taste bitter foods best on the back of your tongue. Tea tastes bitter.

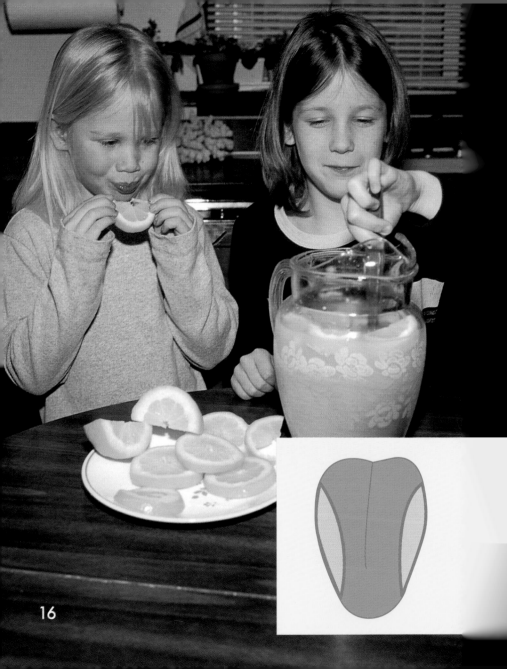

You taste sour foods
best on the sides of
your tongue. A lemon
tastes sour.

You taste some foods on many parts of your tongue. Pizza has many tastes mixed together.

19

Your sense of smell
helps you taste food.
You can smell food
when you taste it.

Words to Know

brain—the organ inside your head that controls your body; your brain understands what your tongue tastes.

detect—to notice something; your taste buds detect flavors.

flavor—the kind of taste in a food

sense—a way of knowing about your surroundings; taste is one of the five senses.

signal—a message; your taste buds send signals to your brain.

taste buds—parts of the tongue with sensors to taste food; bumps on your tongue are called papillae; taste buds are inside each papillae; people are born with about 10,000 taste buds.

Read More

Ballard, Carol. *How Do We Taste and Smell?* How Your Body Works. Austin, Texas: Raintree Steck-Vaughn, 1998.

Frost, Helen. *Your Senses.* The Senses. Mankato, Minn.: Pebble Books, 2000.

Hurwitz, Sue. *Taste.* Library of the Five Senses and the Sixth Sense. New York: PowerKids Press, 1997.

Pluckrose, Henry Arthur. *Eating and Tasting.* Senses. Austin, Texas: Raintree Steck-Vaughn, 1998.

Internet Sites

Taste
http://faculty.washington.edu/chudler/chtaste.html

Tasting
http://sln.fi.edu/qa97/me12/me12.html

Your Sense of Taste
http://tqjunior.advanced.org/3750/taste/taste.html

Index/Word List

Word Count: 141
Early-Intervention Level: 12

Editorial Credits
Mari C. Schuh, editor; Timothy Halldin, cover designer; Kevin T. Kes, illustrator;
  Kimberly Danger, photo researcher

Photo Credits
David F. Clobes, 1, 4, 10, 12, 16, 18, 20
Index Stock Imagery, 8
Leslie O'Shaughnessy, 6
Meggy Becker, 14
Uniphoto, cover